I love reading

Amazing Dinosaur Facts

by Leonie Bennett

Consultant: Luis M. Chiappe, Ph.D.
Director of the Dinosaur Institute
Natural History Museum of Los Angeles County

BEARPORT
PUBLISHING

NEW YORK, NEW YORK

Credits

Cover, Title Page: ticktock Media archive; 4–5: Natural History Museum; 7, 9, 11, 24: Brian Edwards; 10: Simon Mendez; 12–13: Joe Tucciarone/Photo Researchers, Inc.; 14: Lisa Alderson; 17, 20–21, 22B: Luis Rey; 18–19: Chris Tomlin; 21T, 22T: NASA; 23: Shutterstock.

Every effort has been made by ticktock Entertainment Ltd. to trace copyright holders. We apologize in advance for any omissions. We would be pleased to insert the appropriate acknowledgments in any subsequent edition of this publication.

Library of Congress Cataloging-in-Publication Data

Bennett, Leonie.
 Amazing dinosaur facts / by Leonie Bennett.
    p. cm. — (I love reading. Dino world!)
 Includes bibliographical references and index.
 ISBN-13: 978-1-59716-546-4 (library binding)
 ISBN-10: 1-59716-546-8 (library binding)
 1. Dinosaurs—Juvenile literature. 2. Dinosaurs—Miscellanea—Juvenile literature. I. Title.

 QE861.5.B445 2008
 567.9—dc22
                              2007017656

Copyright © 2007 ticktock Entertainment Ltd.
2 Orchard Business Centre, North Farm Road, Tunbridge Wells, Kent, TN2 3XF, UK

Published in the United States of America by Bearport Publishing Company, Inc.
United States text copyright © 2008 Bearport Publishing Company, Inc.

For more information, write to Bearport Publishing Company, Inc., 101 Fifth Avenue, Suite 6R, New York, New York 10003. Printed in the United States of America.

10 9 8 7 6 5 4 3 2 1

Contents

A big dinosaur

Seismosaurus was one of the biggest dinosaurs.

It weighed more than 50 elephants.

Seismosaurus
(*size*-moh-SOR-uhss)

Seismosaurus grew up to 130 feet (40 m) long.

It was longer than three school buses.

A small dinosaur

Microraptor was one of the smallest dinosaurs.

It was about as small as a crow.

It had feathers on its arms, legs, and tail.

It couldn't fly, but it might have glided from tree to tree.

Microraptor
(*mye*-kro-RAP-tur)

tail

feathers

7

A big meat-eater

Giganotosaurus may have been the biggest meat-eating dinosaur.

It was bigger than *Tyrannosaurus rex*.

Some of its teeth were 8 inches (20 cm) long.

Even though *Giganotosaurus* was big, its brain was as small as a grapefruit.

Giganotosaurus
(jig-ah-*not*-oh-SOR-uhss)

9

A big brain

Troodon was a small dinosaur but it had a big brain.

It may have been the smartest dinosaur.

Troodon had long legs that helped it move quickly.

legs

**Troodon
(TROH-oh-don)**

Sails

Spinosaurus was a huge meat-eating dinosaur.

It had a sail on its back.

The sail may have helped it stay cool by getting rid of some heat.

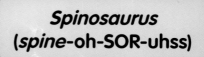

Spinosaurus
(*spine*-oh-**SOR**-uhss)

Little terror

Eoraptor was one of the first meat-eating dinosaurs.

It was small—only about 1.6 feet (.5 m) tall.

Eoraptor
(*ee-oh-RAP-tur*)

Tyrannosaurus rex lived on Earth many years after *Eoraptor.*

It looked like *Eoraptor,* but it was much bigger!

Eoraptor   Tyrannosaurus rex   Human

An unusual head

Olorotitan had a **crest** on top of its head.

Scientists think it might have used the crest for making a loud sound.

Olorotitan was about 30 feet (9 m) long.

It was longer than a dump truck.

crest

Olorotitan
(oh-loh-ROH-ti-tan)

17

Pterosaurs

Pterosaurs were not dinosaurs.

They were **reptiles** that lived at the same time as dinosaurs.

Pterosaurs could fly.

They did not have feathers, but some were covered with hair.

tail

Their wings were made mostly of skin and muscle.

wing

pterosaur
(TERR-uh-*sor*)

19

A dinosaur in space

Coelophysis was a fast runner.

It ate small animals such as **lizards**.

Coelophysis
(*see*-loh-FYE-sis)

Astronauts took a *Coelophysis* skull on a space shuttle.

They thought it would be fun to take a dinosaur into space!

Glossary

astronauts
(ASS-truh-*nawts*)
people who travel
in space

crest (KREST)
feathers or skin
on top of an
animal's head

lizards (LIZ-urdz)
types of animals
with scaly bodies
and tails

reptiles (REP-tilez)
cold-blooded animals
such as lizards, snakes,
or crocodiles

scientists (SYE-uhn-tists)
people who study nature
and the world

23

Index

Read More

Cohen, Daniel.
Dinosaur Discovery:
Facts, Fossils, and Fun!
New York: Puffin (1998).

Zimmerman, Howard.
Dinosaurs!: The Biggest,
Baddest, Strangest, Fastest.
New York: Atheneum (2000).

Learn More Online

To learn more about the world of dinosaurs, visit
www.bearportpublishing.com/ILoveReading